TH

A Tee

Third version

Cartoons by Dave Kirwan
reprinted with special permission
from Carlson & Kirwan Inc.,
Duluth, Minnesota

Cartoons by Randy Glasbergen
reprinted with special permission
from www.glasbergen.com

For information, contact
Dan Celentano
Route 2, Box 402
Sturgeon Lake, MN 55783

Printed in the United States of America

To my friend J.C.

INTRODUCTION

The Garbage

It's where you can put many
of the ideas society has
about what makes you
a valuable person.

People in television,
magazines, the movies –
even people in your school hallways –
would have you believe that all your value
as a human being is wrapped up in your
body.

They say
your body must ***look*** a certain way
or you won't be popular.

They say
you must ***do*** certain things
or you won't be "cool" or have friends.

They say
people's value is determined by
how many friends they have.

I say
this is all ***garbage***.

I say
your value as a person goes a lot deeper
than your skin,

and this book will show you why.

In it are simple facts that tell you exactly
where your value lies and why it is

impossible to have a personality
no one will like.

But before we begin,
let me take out the trash.

WHERE TO FIND IT

WHERE TO FIND IT

CHAPTER 1

THE TOWN OF SHELBY

The back of the school bus was Casey's favorite place to sit ... not just the back, but the last seat, next to the window. That was Casey's seat, and everybody knew it.

It wasn't that this particular seat was any safer or more comfortable than the others. In fact, "comfortable" would be the last word Casey would use to describe it.

It was just that the corner seat was a place for Casey to get away from everyone. It was a place for her to hide.

Casey was a loner, an outsider. She kept pretty much to herself. She bothered no one, and no one really paid much attention to her.

Usually she would just fall asleep until she got to school, her head resting against the window.

Casey's parents had divorced about two years earlier after her father just up and left the family. This weighed heavy on her mind. She blamed herself for her dad leaving. She didn't exactly know why, but she must've had something to do with it.

Ever since the divorce, Casey had turned within herself and shut everyone else out of her life. As much as she wanted friends, as much as she wanted people to like her,

she had lost all confidence in who she was and in her ability to have any friends.

"Dad must not care about me," she figured, *"and I'm sure no one else does either.*

"So, everybody, just leave me alone."

Those were hard times for Casey. If it weren't for Pop being there when she needed him, no telling what would've happened.

"Pop" was her bus driver's nickname. Nobody really knew what his real name was. In fact, every once in a while, Casey would try to get him to tell her.

But he never would.

Instead, he'd always say the same thing to Casey:

"When I'm ready to tell someone, you'll be the first to know."

As much as Casey wondered about Pop's real name,

Pop wondered why Casey was always alone. It just didn't make any sense to him.

Pop wasn't much for words, but from time to time, he'd try to talk to her about this.

"You're a tough kid, Casey," he would say.

"Shoot, I'd put you up against many of the boys in your school. But when it comes to taking on the toughest challenge of your life, you back down.

"You have everything it takes to be somebody, Casey, but you refuse to believe it.
It's your choice, kid,
but I think you deserve better."

Of course Casey never believed Pop when he told her things like that. She thought Pop was just trying to make her feel good.

Every time Pop would have this talk with Casey, she would just nod her head, then quickly change the subject.

Morning after morning, Casey trudged back to her seat, dropped her backpack on the seat next to her, plopped into her place, rested her head against the window, and fell asleep.

It became routine for her.

But as Casey was about to find out, routines sometimes have a way of changing.

And this routine was about to change in a most unusual way.

It happened on a boring Monday, of all days.

Casey headed for her seat as usual, dropped her backpack on the seat next to her, plopped into her place, rested her head against the window, and immediately dozed off.

When the old bus arrived at school, the squeaking of the brakes woke Casey up as it did every morning.

She stretched a bit and glanced past the window as she opened her eyes and reached for her backpack. When she turned to look out the window again, she saw something peculiar. A small group of kids her age were waving at her and motioning her to come off the empty bus.

Casey rubbed her eyes to get a better look.

"Who are those people?" she thought as she quickly turned away in shyness. *"Why are they waving at me?"*

Casey sneaked another look. Maybe they'd be gone. Maybe they were waving at some-body else. But they weren't.

Casey pointed to herself as if to say, "Me? You want me?"

The group nodded in agreement.

Casey laid her backpack down, slowly got up from her seat, and walked to the front of the bus.

"I don't know them," she kept saying to herself. *"Why do they want me? I don't know those kids."*

When she came to the bus steps, she stopped and turned toward the driver's seat. There was Pop.

"Who are those people, Pop?" Casey asked.

Pop smiled at her, but he said nothing. Casey turned back to the kids outside the open bus door.

"You want me?" she asked.

The kids again motioned for her to come with them.

"Come on, Casey," one called. "Come with us."

Casey cautiously started down the steps.

A boy with red hair and a nice smile did most of the talking.

"Hi, Casey! How ya doing?" he said. "Good to see you again."

Everyone in the group agreed.

"Good to see me again?" Casey asked with a confused look on her face.

"Who are you? How do you know my name? I don't know any of you. Where am I?"

"Don't you know?" the red-haired boy said. "You're in Shelby. You know where Shelby is. You've been in Shelby all your life. We're your friends. Don't you remember anything?"

Casey still looked confused.

"What the heck are they talking about?" she asked herself. *"What's going on here? My friends? Been in Shelby all my life?"*

"Come on," a girl from the group said, interrupting Casey's thoughts. "We're going to get something to eat, and we want you to come with us, Casey. Come on."

Again, everyone in the group agreed.

Casey slowly shook her head back and forth.

"No," she said. "I … I can't go with you. I don't know who you are. You've got the wrong person. You don't know me, so you can't like me. Nobody likes me."

Now it was the group's turn to look confused.

Casey paused again, then said, "I have to get back on the bus. I'll be late for school. I've got to go."

"Wait," the red-haired boy said. "You know us. You just don't remember. Come with us, Casey. You won't be late. We really want you to come."

"No," Casey said as she backed up the steps. "You don't know me. Nobody knows me. I … I've got to go."

Casey quickly walked to the back of the bus and huddled in her usual seat.

Suddenly a deep voice interrupted Casey's sleep. This time it wasn't the people at the bottom of the steps. It was Pop.

"Come on," he said.
"Come on, Casey, wake up. You're going to be late for school if you don't get going."

Casey slowly opened her eyes and looked at Pop.

"Pop!" she said. "Where did those kids go? Who are they?"

"You all right, Casey?" he asked. "You better get going. It's 8:15."

Casey paused a moment. She realized that she must've been dreaming. Then reality set in.

"8:15? Did you say 8:15, Pop? I'm gonna be late!"

She quickly grabbed her backpack and ran off the bus.

All day long at school, Casey thought about that morning and how real it had all seemed. She could hardly think of anything else.

On the one hand, she knew it was probably just some silly dream.

But on the other hand, her feeling of having been wanted and accepted by those people was so strong. She had never felt like that before. It was strange, but it was a good feeling to have.

By day's end, though, a sad, lonely feeling had crept deep into Casey's soul. How she wished the people from Shelby had been more than just a dream.

The next morning, Casey hurried to her usual seat on the bus. *"I wonder if I could,"* she thought as she sat down. *"I wonder if I could go back to that town."*

Before she knew it, she was asleep, her head against the window.

Shortly after, Casey woke up and looked out the window. Sure enough, there were all her "friends" motioning to her to get off the bus.

This time she didn't hesitate. Casey raced to the front of the empty bus, stopping only long enough to glance at the driver's seat. There was Pop. Once again, he just smiled.

Casey turned back toward the door and slowly walked down the steps to greet her "friends."

"Come on, Casey! Come with us today," the boy with the red hair said.

"Yeah, Casey, come with us. We want you to be with us," another of the kids said.

"Where are we going?" Casey asked.

"We're gonna get something to eat, then walk around Shelby. We're just gonna mess around and have some fun."

Though she still didn't understand, Casey wasn't about to resist this time.

"Let's do it," she said,
and all were off to Shelby.

Everyone Casey met as she and her friends walked down the quiet, tree-lined streets of Shelby seemed to know her.

Everyone.

It was the most incredible, most gratifying experience she had ever had.

No matter where she went,

whether it was to someone's house,

or to the mall,

or just hanging out at the corner store,

Casey was overwhelmed by the way everyone treated her, by the respect and warmth they showed her. It was so easy to be in Shelby, to just be herself, to laugh again.

It had been such a long time since she had felt like this. It reminded her of those Christmas days when her dad was home and her family was together.

It was exactly
what she had been searching for all her life.

Each school day now, Casey hurried to her usual seat on the bus in anticipation of spending time with her friends in Shelby.

And each day, her friends would be there to greet her. When Casey saw them, she'd rush to the front of the bus, glance at Pop, then join her friends.

But one day before she left the bus, she gave Pop a long look. She just had to ask:

"Pop, I … I don't understand what's going on here. These people – why do they like me so much? I didn't do anything to get them to like me."

Pop smiled his usual "Pop" smile, then he answered Casey:

"Respect and friendship from others are not things you need to earn, Casey. They're things that come from just being who you are.

"Shelby's been trying to tell you this. Shelby's been trying to tell you this for a long time."

Casey lowered her head in thought for a moment. Then she turned to step off the bus, glancing back at Pop one more time.

"*This is crazy,*" she thought, shaking her head.

There was no doubt Casey enjoyed her friends' company, and they enjoyed hers. She had never received this kind of attention and affection from anyone in her life.

But the same questions kept nagging her:
"What's going on here?
Why do these people like me?"

Casey was determined to get some answers. If Pop couldn't give them to her, maybe her friends could.

One day, while having lunch at the mall with her friends, she decided to give it a try.

Sitting across from her in the booth was the red-haired boy. Both were waiting for the rest of the group to get their food.

Casey spoke up:

"Hey, umm, maybe you can help me out," she said to the red-haired boy as she nervously moved things around on her tray. "I, ahhh, I just can't understand something. I don't understand what's going on here.

"What am I doing here? Why does everybody like me? I don't understand. I'm no great athlete or nothing. I'm certainly not the best-looking person in the world, that's for sure. What's going on here?"

The red-haired boy unwrapped his burger, smoothed out the paper, then looked up at Casey to answer her.

“You don’t have to do nothing for us. We just like you, that’s all. We just like you.”

There was a pause while the boy took a small bite out of his burger.

Shortly after, he spoke up again. This time he stared straight into Casey's eyes.

“Don’t you get it, Casey?” he said. “All these things happening to you – they are all things Shelby’s been trying to tell you.

“They are all things Shelby has been trying to tell you for a long time.

“This is what Shelby is really all about.”

Casey slowly leaned back in her booth.

“Shelby’s been trying to tell me this for a long time,” she thought.

“He’s worse than Pop.”

Casey may not have understood what was going on, but she did know she wanted to be in Shelby.

There, the sun was always shining, and every day was as warm as the people she was with.

She enjoyed her friends' company, and

– surprisingly, Casey thought –

they enjoyed hers.

She had rarely gotten this kind of attention and affection from anyone in her life.

Gradually Casey's thoughts
of worthlessness
were worn down by her feelings
of confidence and happiness.

She wished she could stay in Shelby forever.

Then came the day Casey feared most.

Casey rushed to her corner seat as usual, tossed her backpack next to her, and fell asleep as she always did.

But this day, when the squeaking of the brakes woke her up, she wasn't in Shelby.

Casey frantically looked out the window.

"What happened?" she asked herself. *"Where are they? Where are my friends?"*

Casey grew anxious.

She tried to go back to sleep again and again, but to no avail. Every time she woke up, no one was there.

"Casey," Pop called as he looked into the huge rearview mirror. "It's time to go. Come on, you're gonna be late."

Casey didn't answer.

"Casey? You all right? You better get going. You're gonna be late."

Still no answer.

Pop walked to the back of the bus to see what was going on.

"Casey, what are you doing?" he asked. "You all right?"

Casey opened her eyes.

"Pop," she asked, "where are those kids?"

"What are you talking about, Casey?" Pop said. "You better get going. I have to get the bus back to the garage, and you have to go to school."

"Pop," she insisted, "you know what I'm talking about. The kids I've been hanging out with – where are they?"

"Casey, you're not making any sense. You just had a dream or something. You better get going, or you're gonna be late."

"Pop...." Casey slowly lowered her head in disappointment. She knew Pop was right.

There would be no Shelby today.

In fact, there was no Shelby the rest of the week.

As hard as she tried to bring it back, she couldn't.

Every day, Casey rushed to her seat, dropped her backpack next to her, and fell asleep in hopes of being with her Shelby friends.

But nothing.

Shelby was gone. The love and affection she had felt in that brief moment of time was gone.

It had all disappeared.

The school bus stopped in front of Casey's house as it did every Friday afternoon.

She got off the bus, but instead of heading for her house, she walked to her favorite "getaway" spot, which was in a small alley behind Buck's grocery store.

There, alone, she leaned her back against the cement wall, dropped her backpack, and slid down the wall to the ground.

She pulled her knees up close to her body and rested her arms across them.

"Shelby," she thought to herself.
"Where are you?
Where in the heck did you go?"

Casey was deep in thought about Shelby when she was interrupted by the sound of footsteps coming toward her.

She lifted her head, trying to focus her eyes.

As the figure came closer, Casey recognized him.

It was Pop.

"Pop," Casey said, surprised to see him. "What are you doing here?"

"Shortcut to my house from the store. What are you doing here?"

Casey rested her chin on her arms. "Just thinking."

Pop pulled an old wooden crate close to him and slowly sat down on it. He placed his small bag of groceries on the ground next to the crate.

"What are you thinking about?"
he asked gently.

Casey's thoughts flew around in her head:
"Should I tell him?
Should I tell him about what happened?
I really don't want to tell anyone.
Maybe he'll think I'm crazy or something.
I think I'm crazy or something.

"But if I can't trust Pop, who can I trust?
I just gotta tell someone."

Casey wiggled a bit to get more comfortable. Then she spoke: "Well, this is going to sound stupid to you, Pop, but here goes."

And Casey began to tell her story....

"… and when I woke up, I was in this beautiful town with all these really nice people. Everybody in town knew me, Pop, and they were real nice to me – especially the kids. It was like they had known me forever. I never felt so good in all my life. I felt like I was somebody important, somebody special. I didn't even have to try. I wish I really had friends like that."

Casey paused as she eased back into her original sitting position.

"And then one day I woke up and nothing. No town, no people, no friends, no nothing. Just like it is today.

"Just like it's been forever.

"This may sound silly to you, Pop, but I miss that town. I miss those people really bad. I wish I could go back. I wish I could see them again."

There was a pause as Pop fiddled with his groceries. Then he asked Casey an odd question:

"What's the name of this town you were in?"

Casey stared at the ground for a moment in thought:

"He wants to know the name of the town?
Here I am, telling him all this personal stuff,
and he wants to know the name of the town?
He must think I'm really nuts."

"Never mind, Pop," Casey said aloud as she slowly raised her head. "I talked too much already. I feel embarrassed enough as it is. Let's just drop the whole thing."

Silence hung in the air between them.

Pop picked up his bag of groceries and slowly stood up.

"Casey," he said,
"soon you will understand
what I've been trying to tell you for so long.

"Soon you will understand."

Pop said nothing more.

Casey looked confused.

"What the heck is he talking about?"
she asked herself.

*"Man, I hope he's not mad at me
or anything."*

As Pop began to walk away, Casey spoke up.

"Hey, Pop, come on!
Why don't you tell me your real name?"
she asked, trying to lighten things up.

Pop turned and smiled as he always did when Casey asked him that question, but this time, something was different. There was a long pause before Pop answered, and the way he said it was different from all the other times.

"When I'm ready to tell someone,
you'll be the first to know."

This made Casey wonder
if something might be wrong with Pop.

"What's up, Pop? You all right?"

Pop adjusted the groceries under his arm and once again slowly walked away without saying another word.

Casey watched as he left the alley.

She had a lot to think about that day. It was dark when she finally decided to go home.

Monday morning came too quickly for Casey. She had spent much of the weekend thinking about Shelby and what Pop had said.

It was tough to get going, but eventually she was ready for school. Grabbing her back-pack, she said goodbye to her mom and headed for the bus.

The bus was late. Pop was never late.

Finally, it arrived, and the door swung open.

"Hey, Pop! Where've you been?"
Casey said as she started up the steps.

"Wait a minute. You're not Pop."

"No," the new bus driver said sadly.
"I'm Donna."

"Where's Pop?" Casey asked.

Donna paused before answering.

"He passed away this weekend in his sleep," she said in a soft voice. "I'm sorry."

Casey froze. "Pop? Dead?" she asked in disbelief. "That can't be. I was just talking to him a few days ago. He was fine."

The driver slowly hung her head, saying nothing more about it.

Casey's body was numb. Pop's death cut deeply into her very soul. Ever since she could remember, Pop had always been there for her.

Casey slowly turned and started to trudge to her seat. As she did, the bus driver spoke up.

"Uh, excuse me. You wouldn't happen
to be Casey, would you?"

Casey looked back and nodded as she quickly wiped a tear from her cheek.

"My boss asked me to give you this envelope."

Casey absent-mindedly took the envelope and stuck it in her back pocket before heading to the back of the bus.

If there had been a seat on the back bumper, she would've gladly taken it. More than ever, she wanted to be alone.

Casey stared out the window as tears streamed down her face. As fast as the tears came, she'd wipe them away, not wanting anyone to see her cry. She couldn't believe Pop was gone.

Seems like everyone she had ever loved – her father, her friends in Shelby, and now Pop – had disappeared from her life.

It was a long day at school. The ride home was quiet.

As Casey stepped off the bus, she again decided to head for her thinking spot in the alley. This time she ran.

When she got there, she threw her backpack on the ground and immediately slid down the wall to sit. She pulled her knees up close to her body, wrapped her arms around her legs, and rested her forehead on her knees.

Tears streamed from her eyes as she thought about Pop. *"Why did you have to go, Pop?"* she thought. *"Why did you have to go?"*

After a while, Casey remembered the envelope she'd been given on the bus.

She pulled it from her back pocket and smoothed it out. She slowly opened it, took out a letter, and started to read.

The letter was short and to the point.

Casey,

Never forget:

Friendship and respect from others
are not things you need to earn.
They're things that come
by just being who you are.

I've been trying to tell you this.
I've been trying to tell you this
for a long time.

Now you know.

Your friend always,

Shelby

"Shelby?" she whispered to herself. "What the heck is going on here?"

Then it hit her.

"Shelby! Pop's real name is Shelby!"

A cold chill slowly crept into her body.

It was then she remembered what the red-haired boy had told her in the mall restaurant:

"All these things happening to you … they are all things Shelby's been trying to tell you.

"They are all things Shelby's been trying to tell you for a long time."

Casey lifted up her eyes in deep thought.

"'*Things Shelby's been trying to tell me,*'" she whispered.

"Could it be? But how?

"How could he ...?"

What Casey was thinking just didn't seem possible.

But it was.

You see, Shelby wasn't about any town.

It was more than that …

much more.

You might say Shelby was Pop's farewell gift
to Casey before he died,
his way of saying to her:

*"If you didn't understand me
when I tried to tell you,*

maybe you'd understand if I showed you."

And show her he did.

In a strange, eerie turn of events
that could have been taken
right from the pages of "The Twilight Zone,"

Shelby the town

was really the *words* of Shelby the man

played out for Casey right in front of her eyes.

It was everything Pop (or Shelby) had been
trying to tell Casey for years.

And everything he'd been trying to tell her
was now beginning to make sense.

That is ...

Within your soul
truly lies everything needed
to be <u>somebody</u>.

It's been there all the time.
You need to do nothing to earn it.

And
simply enough,

it comes by just being who you are.

"Man,"
Casey said as she carefully folded the letter.

"This is unbelievable.
Nobody is every going to believe this."

She slowly worked her way up the wall
to stand.

Before she left the alley,
she opened the letter
and read it one more time.

"Nobody is every going to believe this
in a million years."

Every once in a while, Casey would still sit in the alley behind Buck's grocery store and think about all that had happened to her in the past few months and how much of an impact it had on her life.

One day while sitting there deep in thought, she was suddenly interrupted by a friendly voice.

"We knew we'd find you here," a boy said.

Casey looked up. It was a few kids she had met at the high school she was attending this year.

"Come on," the boy said.
"We're going to town. Quit sitting around, and come with us."

Casey stretched out her hand.

"Help me up," she said.

The boy with red hair and a nice smile grabbed Casey's hand, gave a tug, and pulled her to her feet.

Casey steadied herself. She then paused a moment to give the boy a hard look.

"Whaaat?" the boy asked,
staring back at Casey.

"Ya know," she said, "I … I still can't get over how much you look like someone I used to know."

Casey's friends looked at one another as if to say, "Aw, man. Here we go again."

"Yeah, well," the boy with red hair said as they all started to walk away,

"you've told me that a million times.

"And before you ask me again,
the answer is 'No.'

"I ain't never been to a place called Shelby."

There was a pause before Casey spoke up:

"Nice place, Shelby is."

Casey's words echoed off the buildings in the empty alley as the group walked away.

"Nice place."

THE MANY ROADS TO SHELBY

Everyone searches for the town of Shelby
in his or her life.

Everyone.

From the big, bad, “tough guy”
who tries to find it in a gang

to the lonely teenager
who drifts into seclusion,

from the person who uses drugs

to the student who tries to do the right thing,

everyone wants to feel like

somebody to **someone**.

But even though we **all** search for the town
of Shelby, not everyone is able to find it.

That’s because some of the roads
people take in their search lead only
to dried-up riverbeds

or

to empty fields long overgrown
with weeds and small trees.

These roads are dead ends.

In the next few sections are
some of the dead-end roads people take
in their search for Shelby.

Hopefully, they will serve as examples
of roads you won't want to take.

THE PERFORMER

You're sitting on the front steps of your house "shooting the breeze" with a friend.

You talk about this.
You talk about that.
No big deal.

Suddenly, while talking about some of the people you know, your friend says something that takes you totally by surprise.

"Yeah," your friend says, "he said
he doesn't like you. But don't worry about it."

You pause before you respond:

"Why did he say that?"

"I don't know, but I heard other people say it,
too. They said you act stupid or something.
I don't know. It's no big thing.
Don't worry about it."

Even though you're stunned about what was said, you still try to be "cool" about the whole situation. The last thing you want to do is to show your friend that it really bothers you.

"Yeah?" you say, lifting your chin a little.
"Do you think that bothers me?
Well, it doesn't. I couldn't care less
what those creeps think about me.
It ain't no big thing. It doesn't bother me."

After a while, your friend leaves.

At this point you start thinking
pretty seriously about what was said.

Now it's up to you.
What do you think about?

How much would it bother you
that there are people in your school
who **really don't like you**?

Would it be any big thing to you?

Would you have enough confidence in your-self to just shrug it off and forget all about it?
Or
would you **panic**?

Would you start thinking about changing who you are just to get people to notice you more?

Would you, for example, start to question
how you **look**?

Would you start to question how heavy you are

or the clothes you wear

or the way you look
every time you see yourself in the mirror?

Or maybe you wouldn't question
your looks at all.

Maybe you feel it's the things you DO that
must change. Maybe you think
that you're just not "cool" enough.

Maybe you think that doing certain "cool"
things will get people to like you more –

maybe things like doing drugs

or drinking alcohol

or skipping class

or putting people down

or cursing all the time

or stealing

or joining a gang.

They're all "cool," right?

Well, maybe not.
But at least they'll get people to look at you.

After all, everybody knows that if you do
dumb things to try to get attention,

people are going to look!

If you don't believe it,
try doing this with a rubber hose,

and see how many people look at you.

They'll look for sure.

But what are they looking at?

The guy with the hose is getting attention,
but what is the attention based on?

Is it based on WHO HE IS,
or
is it based on WHAT HE'S **DOING**?

Big difference!

People will definitely give you attention when you do dumb things,

but they **won't** give you something
that is far more valuable –

RESPECT.

Make no mistake about it,

as long as it doesn't hurt yourself
or anyone else,

there's nothing wrong with wanting to look nice or wanting to be the best at something.

Everybody wants that.

But when you start placing
all your value as a person
on the way you ***look***

or

on the things you ***do***,

you set yourself up for a ***serious*** letdown.

Do you really think that the things you do or the way you look tell people everything they need to know about you?

Doesn't your value as a person go a lot deeper than your skin?

I sure hope so.

If not,
I could only imagine
the frustration and anger you would feel
if you ever found yourself
in a situation such as David was in.

David was a kid who was stripped of every sense of **outer identity** he had as a person.

He had no **looks** to speak of because of the burns on his face.

He was in no shape to **do** anything because of the deformities he suffered.

But in spite of all this,
David was the most popular kid in the country.

He was so popular, in fact, they made a movie about his experiences.

"But how can this be?" you might ask.

"How can someone be popular
if he has no looks
and
is in no shape to do anything
with his friends?"

The story of David is incredible.

The evening was chilly in more ways than one when 6-year-old David and his father pulled up to the door of their motel room.

David's parents were going through a bitter divorce, and there was no way his father would let him live with his mother.

It was late. David was tired and went right to bed after he got into the room. His father sat in a chair next to him and waited.

When the little boy was fast asleep, his father slowly rose from the chair, went out to the car, opened the trunk, and pulled out a can of kerosene.

When he was back in the room, he checked one more time to make sure David was soundly asleep.

He was.

His father then opened the can, sprinkled the kerosene around his little son on the bed, and lit a match. The flickering flame reflected the anger in his eyes as he mumbled to David:

"If I can't have you, son, neither will your mother."

Then he threw the lighted match onto the bed and walked out the door.

The tiny flame burst into a blaze.

The bedspread caught on fire.

David's clothes caught on fire.

David rolled to the floor in fear as he tried to put out the flames that engulfed his body.

Firefighters eventually came and quickly wrapped blankets around the boy, smothering the flames.

David survived.

But he was in bad shape.

Most of his body was badly burned. His fingers were nubs, and what was left of his hair looked like little strands of thread.

His face was so bad that he had to wear a skin-grafting mask to help with the healing.

Everything that **society says** is valuable to humans was taken away from David.

He had no **looks** to speak of

and was obviously in no shape to **do** anything.

If our value as human beings were based solely on how we **look**

or on the things we **do**,

David would have absolutely no value as a person. He would be a useless hunk of flesh left to curl up in a ball, wither, and die.

Thank goodness our value
as human beings
goes a lot deeper than that.

This was made clear a few years later when David's mom called a news conference to let the public know how he was doing.

The television news conference was held in a large room where a crowd of reporters gathered to hear what this boy had to say.

A long table was set up in front of the room, and a dozen or so microphones were grouped in front of a chair where David was to sit.

After a time, David slowly made his way in from the right side of the room. He painfully walked toward the microphones, aided by a nurse who gently held his right arm for support. David carefully sat down in front of the microphones as the reporters began to ask him questions.

In answering them, David was "cool." He could have easily let his anger and hatred for what his father did do all the talking for him, but he didn't.

David was simply David.

He was confident. He was strong. And he communicated in such a manner that made the country fall in love with him.

Everything that truly defined who David really was as a person came through loud and clear that evening.

When I first saw this boy come into the room,

the mask,
the burn scars,
the nubs on his hands instead of fingers,

I heard people attach a name to his body:

"David."

Putting one and one together,
his **looks** and his **name,**

I knew that this was a **human being**
named **David**.

That was it … nothing more, nothing less.

But then I heard and saw David communicate with others. I listened to him as he answered the reporters' questions. I saw him afterward, interacting with others on stage.

It was then I could see that this wasn't
just a human being,

but a human being who was
strong, confident, intelligent, forgiving
and who had a good sense of humor.

This is when I got to know David **the person**,

and David **the person** was a great kid.

“So,”

you might ask,

“what does this all have to do with me?”

Well, maybe nothing.

But if there ever comes a time in your life when you see a need to change who you are just because you don’t like the way you **look**

or because you don’t feel you’re **as good as everyone else**,

think about the story of David, then tell me your changes are really going to make a difference.

They won’t.

That's because like David,

like anyone,

the greatest power you have

in making friends,

going out on dates,

and drawing people to you in general

will always come from within your body,

not from without.

That's something that will never change.

David never got caught up
in what society had to say
as to what made him a valuable person.

He didn't even get caught up
in what some people in his school had to say.

And for all those who **like and respect** David,

they're sure glad he didn't.

THE STREET PUPPET

STREET PUPPETS are people who feel that the only way they can ever be accepted by anyone is to just go along with "the crowd" when "the crowd" wants them to do something wrong.

It doesn't matter how dumb this wrong thing may be.

It doesn't matter how harmful it may be.

It doesn't matter how ridiculous it may appear.

The street puppets' goal is to be accepted, and they will do just about anything to see that it happens.

It's too bad that people who get easily misled by their friends don't understand that one's **value** as an individual is **not** based on **performance**,

but rather on **character**.

Anthony sure didn't understand this.

The true story of Anthony is a good example of how easy it is for some people to get trapped into doing things they really don't want to do – just to be accepted by their friends.

Anthony was a slender 16-year-old boy who never thought he'd find himself in the kind of trouble he was in.

After all, he had never even been sent to the principal's office much less to a juvenile jail.

As he stood looking out the narrow window from his cramped cell, Anthony kept asking himself the same questions over and over again.

"What am I doing here?"

"How did I get into this mess?"

"How did this happen?"

Anthony's problems started when his family moved from North Carolina to a small town in Minnesota. He was new to his high school and really wanted to be accepted.

One day, a small group of boys

came up to Anthony and asked him if he wanted to go to a beer party that evening. Anthony had never been drinking before in his life.

He didn't like the taste of the stuff
and never saw a need
to do something he didn't like
just to hang out with friends.

But because he wanted to be accepted in his new school, Anthony put aside all that for now and agreed to go to the party.

At the party, Anthony drank just one can of beer. Even that was tough for him to take.

But Anthony's drinking just one can of beer didn't stop his "friends" from asking him to go to another party.

He went to that party and drank,

then to another party and drank,

and to still another party and drank.

It got to a point where Anthony wasn't drinking just one can of beer anymore.

He was drinking a six-pack

and some vodka

and some rum.

Anthony liked hanging out with his new friends. Even though they did things that were totally against what he believed in,

hanging out with these people gave Anthony

a sense of importance,

of acceptance,

like he was **somebody** special or something.

Anthony actually believed that the people he was hanging out with were the kind of friends who would be there for him if he ever really needed them.

This gave Anthony a feeling of security he had never had before in his life.

But there was also a dark side
to this whole situation.

The boy who'd never been drinking before,

the boy who had always tried
to do the right thing in life,

the boy who had put aside his values
just to be accepted

was now developing
a serious drinking problem.

Anthony was at a point
where he would drink just about anything
his friends put in front of him.

But having a drinking problem was the last thing on Anthony's mind.

Just having someone to hang around with
was all that mattered to him now.

Then came that one evening.

Anthony went to one of his parties as usual. When he walked into the house, he saw his "friends" sitting in a circle on the living room floor.

Thinking nothing of it, Anthony sat with them.

Shortly after he had sat down, someone pulled out a marijuana cigarette,

lit it up, took a drag,

and passed it to the next person in the circle.

This person also took a drag, and so on.

The marijuana got to Anthony. Everyone waited for him to take a drag. He stared at the joint for a moment, then raised his head, and slowly moved his eyes around the circle. As he was doing this, his mind began to race.

"I don't want this garbage," he thought.
"Drinking is messin' me up enough.
I don't want this. No way
am I fooling around with this stuff."

He then passed the joint to the next person without taking a drag.

"What's the matter?" one boy said in a sarcastic tone. "Too strong for you? Want a candy joint instead?"

Everyone in the circle laughed.

"Give me a break, kid,"
another said to Anthony.
"I didn't think you were such a baby."

Suddenly an uneasy feeling crept into Anthony's body. As he looked around, the faces he once knew were no longer familiar, but rather dark shadows of people he had never met before. This made Anthony feel really uncomfortable – so much so that he wanted to leave.

But as Anthony tried to stand up, something peculiar happened:

He couldn't seem to get off the floor.

It was like he was glued to the carpet.

The heavy hand of "rejection" literally held Anthony in place. He was afraid that if he left that party, people would make fun of him, and no one would ever want to hang out with him anymore.

So he stayed.

The marijuana kept going around,
and Anthony kept passing it on.

Suddenly, there was a knock at the door.

"Open up," the voice on the other side said. "It's the police. We got a complaint of too much noise. Open the door."

As everyone scrambled to try to get away, the front door slammed open, and the police came in, arresting everyone for possession of a controlled substance.

As Anthony was being handcuffed, he turned to his friends for support.

"Would someone tell them I didn't do anything? Tell them I didn't do nothing."

Anthony expected his friends to speak up for him.

He actually expected someone to "cover his back." But no one said anything. Some just looked away, while others smirked.

"Come on!" Anthony said in an anxious voice. "Quit messin' around!

"You know I didn't do anything. Tell them! Tell them!"

Once again, silence. The only thing that could be heard was the clicking of the handcuffs.

Anthony slowly hung his head. A look of anger and frustration showed on his face as he was led out the front door.

"All that time wasted,"
he thought.

"All that time wasted
trying to get people to like me.

"And what do I have to show for it?

"A pair of handcuffs,

a drinking problem,

and a bunch of 'coconuts'
I thought were friends."

Anthony served time at Hyland Detention Center, then was sent to an alcohol treatment facility to get help with his drinking problem.

But Anthony's story doesn't end there.

Shortly after, his family moved again – this time to a town in southern Minnesota.

Anthony was new to his high school and wanted to be accepted. One day, a boy from the "in crowd" came up to Anthony's locker and invited him to a beer party.

Anthony raised his head, looked the boy squarely in the eye, and said in a slow, soft, but firm voice:

"A beer party?
I don't want to go to your beer party."

There was a pause as Anthony gathered his books for the next class.

The boy from the "in crowd"
looked at Anthony strangely.

"No," Anthony said again as he put his books in his backpack. "I don't want to go to your party."

Another pause ...

"And if you're smart,"

he said as he closed his locker door,

"you don't want to go either."

BREAKING THE GRIP OF "THE PUPPETEER"

If you feel that you are a street puppet and would like to break the grip "the puppeteer," or "the misleader," has on you, here are a few suggestions:

<u>FIRST</u>

Understand,

I mean **REALLY** understand,

that your value as a person is not based on what your friends
or girl/boy friend
want you to do.

It is based on **who you are** as a person.

The ability to make friends and be accepted already lies within you.

It comes by just being who you are.

Doing dumb things just to please your friends is **not** going to add to that ability in any way.

In fact, it will probably take away from it.

You will **never** break the pull of *"the puppeteer"* unless you truly understand this first point.

<u>SECOND</u>

If your friends don't understand this, then it's time to **let go**.

Quit hanging around people
who have no respect for you as a person.

I know this is a lot easier said than done.
I know that the pull of having people around,
even people who have no respect for you,
is hard to break away from.

But your philosophy should be simple.

That is:

"I'd rather let go
*and be **respected** by a few people*
*than hold on and be **used** by many."*

If you adopt this philosophy in your life and just be yourself, you <u>**will**</u> be respected,

and you will be respected by more than just a few people ...

one person being

YOURSELF.

THE ULTIMATE FRIENDSHIP TEST

Did you ever wonder if the people you hang out with are really good friends? I mean, did you ever wonder if they are people who like **you** for **you** or only for what you **do**
— especially the **wrong** things you do?

Want to find out?

Take
THE ULTIMATE FRIENDSHIP TEST
and see for yourself.

Here's how it works.

Hang out with your friends as usual —
mess around,
have a good time,
enjoy your friendship with them
as you normally do.
After all, they're good friends.

However,
if any of your friends want you to do
something that could really mess you over
in some way —

serious things like
doing drugs, drinking, stealing,
skipping school, or whatever —

do the right thing instead.

"Naa," you say to them, "don't want to go to the party and be drinking and stuff. But give me a call later."

or

"Naa, don't want to skip class. What are you trying to do to me? I'm too far behind as it is. I'll give you a call tonight."

After two weeks of doing this,

look around.

Whoever is still left hanging out with you,

they

are your true friends.

Of course, this test isn't for everyone. That's because most friends won't ask you to do something that will hurt you or mess you over in some way.

But for those of you who do have "friends" like that, you might want to give this little test a try.

I know if Anthony had taken it, he wouldn't have ended up in the mess he was in.

MY FAULT

IT'S ALWAYS MY FAULT

Robert's mom and stepfather are having another big fight
– the second one in just two days.

Robert goes to his room to avoid the conflict. As he closes the door behind him, the yelling gets louder. Robert sits on the edge of his bed.

Lowering his head, he feels frustrated, trapped. He wants to leave, but he doesn't dare step out of his room, afraid that his parents will turn their anger on him.

Robert nervously picks up a comic book from the floor and thumbs through it to take his mind off the argument.

It doesn't help.

In fact, he tosses the comic aside, gets up, and locks his bedroom door to help him feel more secure.

Robert begins to wonder what's going on.

"Why are they fighting now?" he mumbles. "They're always fighting. I'm sick of it."

Suddenly, the front door slams.
Dad's gone… again.

As quickly as the fight had started, it ends.

An uneasy silence fills the house. Robert waits and listens. He hopes and prays that his mom doesn't call for him.

A second door slams – his parents' bedroom.

"I wonder what happened," he thinks.

"I wonder if it was something I did?

"Me and Sis had another big fight today.

"Maybe that's it.

"Maybe they're sick of us kids always fighting."

A guilty fear creeps into Robert's body as he begins to blame himself for the argument between his mother and stepfather.

As time goes on,
the guilt and the blame get stronger.

"Yeah, that's got to be it. It's either that or … or … my last report card.

"I really messed up on my last report card. They told me they were disappointed in me."

"Maybe that's it. I don't know."

"Whatever it is, it's probably my fault. It's always my fault. I'm such a jerk. I hate myself for all the stupid stuff I do."

"I wish I could just get out of here."

"I wish I could just start over."

"I wish I could just leave forever."

It's always something.

If it wasn't this latest fight between his parents,
it was the divorce.

If it wasn't the divorce,
it was his grandmother's death.
(He happened to be in the room
when she died.)

If it wasn't his grandmother's death,
it was the blame he took for his real father
never coming to visit him.

On and on.

"It's my fault.
It's gotta be my fault.
I'm no good.
And nobody can ever tell me different."

As you can see, Robert has become
a master at playing the "blame game."

Everything bad that happens to him in his
life is always his fault.
He takes on all the guilt.
He takes on all the hurt.
He takes on all the blame.

For what?

Ninety-nine percent of the bad things Robert
blames himself for **weren't even his fault.**

The argument between his parents is a good example of that.

The argument had nothing to do with Robert and everything to do with his stepfather having money problems

and his mother having a drinking problem.

They weren't even talking about him.

But try telling that to Robert.

No way are you going to convince him
that the argument between his parents
had nothing to do with him.

No way are you going to get him to believe
that **other people's problems** sometimes
fall on innocent people.

But it's not surprising
that Robert feels this way.

NO MATTER HOW STUPID IT MAY BE,

there will always be those

who blame themselves for everything bad

that happens to them in their life.

Teenagers are notorious for doing this.

There are those who would
never stop to think that

maybe,

just maybe,

it's not about them,

but about other people with problems.

Could this be possible?

Bet the ranch on it!

But the **"blame game"** is
only half the problem teenagers face
when they start taking responsibility
for other people's problems.

The other half has to do with what is called
"BLENDING."

"BLENDING" is when people combine
the bad things that happen to them
because of other people,

things like divorce, parents arguing all the
time, abuse, or constantly getting yelled at,

with the **amount of value** they already have
as individuals.

You saw a little of this with Robert
when he said:

"**I hate <u>myself</u>** for all the stupid stuff I do."
and
"**What a jerk <u>I</u> am.**"

Not only did Robert take the blame
for his parents' argument,

but he went one step further and
took this blame out on himself **personally**.

One doesn't have to be a rocket scientist to understand the negative impact "blending" can have on a person.

Any first-grader can add 1 and 1:

1 "My parents got a divorce,"

and somehow

+1 "it must be all my fault,"

——— therefore,

= 2 "I must be a bad person."

Remember the story of David?

Obviously, David had some pretty terrible things happen to him because of his father.

He could have easily ***blamed himself*** for what had happened,

but he didn't.

Instead, David was more like:

"You burned the outside of my body
and you hurt me really bad, Dad.
But you ain't gonna be able to touch
who I am on the inside.
That belongs to me."

Unfortunately, too many young people can't seem to do this.

Situations such as divorce, family problems, and physical/sexual abuse become problems teenagers take on ***personally***

instead of problems
put on them by other people.

The bottom line is simple.

When you allow other people's problems to become yours,

when you allow others to make you hate who you are,

you open yourself up to a whole array of personal problems such as

depression,

anger,

loneliness,

insecurity,

self-hatred ....

So if something bad is done **to** you or **around** you that makes you feel really down or depressed, remember these four facts:

1. The "**world of bad**" does not revolve around you. Bad things sometimes happen to innocent people. It isn't always about you, but often about people with problems.

2. Try hard to separate the bad things done to the **outside** of your body from the amount of **value you have as a person** on the inside. They are two different things. ***Bad things*** that happen to you in your life by other people don't make you a ***bad person.***

3. Make sure you find someone to talk to about your problem. Talking over your problems with someone not only helps you to find solutions on how to deal with it, but also releases much of the frustrations you feel about it.

4. If you do something wrong that is your fault, ***you want to take responsibility for it, make it right, and move on with your life.*** No big deal. But when it comes to situations like ***divorce, verbal or sexual abuse, parents' problems, neglect, and others,*** taking the blame is like trying to kill a fly that lands on your nose with a frying pan ....

Not smart.

The only one who gets hurt is you.

THE "BLAME GAME" TEST

Whose fault is it
when something bad happens
to you

or

around you?

Is everything that goes wrong in your life
always your fault?

The following

"BLAME GAME" TEST

may give you some answers.

Here's how it works ….

FIRST

Put yourself in the following story:

Your mom sends you to the store to buy a box of stick matches so she can light the furnace. As you walk home, the box falls out of your shopping bag, and all the matches are scattered on the ground.

Frustrated, you bend down to pick them up. You think you've gotten them all, but a few are still left on the sidewalk.

A short time later, a man recently released from jail for arson comes by. He sees the few wooden matches lying there and decides to use them to get revenge on the person who sent him to jail. He's been wanting to do this for a long time.

He goes to this person's house, lights one of the matches, and sets the house on fire.

It burns to the ground, and the family living there loses everything. Everyone survives, but two of the children are injured.

The next day while listening to the radio, you hear about this tragedy on the news. You learn that the arsonist was caught and arrested. You also learn that the matches he used to start the fire were found on the same street corner where you had dropped yours.

Then it hits you.
A shock goes through your body.

“Those were the matches I dropped,” you say to yourself. “I thought I’d picked them all up, but maybe I didn’t.

“Could it be my fault
the man set the house on fire?

“If I’d made sure I picked up all the matches, maybe those people would still have their home, and no one would have gotten hurt.”

<u>SECOND</u>

Think about
and answer the following questions:

- Would you blame yourself for the fire the arsonist started?

- Would it be your fault that those children were hurt and their family is homeless?

- Do you think the man who started the fire had some problems before he lit the match?

- Did you purposely drop the matches so the man could find them and take his anger out on other people?

- If the man hadn't found the matches and wasn't able to take his anger out on those people at that time,

do you think he eventually would've taken his anger out on someone else?

- Why?

THIRD

Think about the problem that is causing you so much guilt,

the one for which you are constantly blaming yourself.

Take that situation and substitute it for the ***fire*** *in the questions on the previous page.*

In questions where ***"the man"*** *is mentioned, substitute for "the man" the name of the person(s) who hurt you.*

Now, answer the questions again
using both substitutions.

Take your time in doing this.

You may have to shuffle things around a bit to fit your situation, but give it a chance.

Do you get the point now?

Blaming yourself for someone else's problems
is like blaming yourself
for a fire that was set by somebody else.

It makes absolutely no sense.

THE LONER

Ashley is a good kid.

She does well in school, has a part-time job, and she is, without a doubt, the best artist in town.

But not too many people know very much about Ashley. In fact, not too many people even know her name.

You see, like so many other kids, Ashley is considered a "loner,"

an "outsider,"

a person who just doesn't seem to fit in.

Out of all the so-called "cliques" in her school, none seems to be right for her.

Every time she goes to school, she feels like an uninvited guest at a party of strangers.

Often when people need to build themselves up in front of their friends, Ashley is the target of their put-downs.

Ashley can handle it though. She simply looks at the person, gives one of those "cool" smiles she always gives, and then just walks away.

"Nobody even knows who I am,"

Ashley sometimes says to herself.

"But yet they got to be putting me down.
What's wrong with these people?"

Ashley is sometimes hurt by what others say to her, but she eventually shrugs it off and goes on with her life.

I imagine Ashley could easily find a spot in one of the cliques in her school if she really wanted to.

But Ashley isn't stupid.

She knows that in order to "fit in," she probably would have to give up something in return.

Maybe it would mean she'd have to **look** a certain way or **act** a certain way to be accepted.

Maybe it would mean she'd have to do to others what they were doing to her.

Or maybe, just maybe, it would mean she'd have to mess around with drugs or booze to be accepted.

Whatever it would be, Ashley isn't about to change who she is just to be "part of the crowd."

Her attitude is simple:

"Take me as I am, or just leave me alone."

I guess there's a price to pay for having such an attitude. But considering the alternative, Ashley is willing to pay it,

and pay it gladly.

No problem.

Obviously Ashley has a lot of confidence in herself. If she didn't, she wouldn't have the attitude she has.

Ashley is a loner by **choice**. She is the kind of person who probably will end up making some pretty good friends one day simply because she believes in who she is.

But Ashley is only *one type* of loner you'll find in your school.

There's another.

Unfortunately, the other type of loner isn't as confident as Ashley is. In fact, they're just the opposite.

They are people who simply don't like who they are and don't feel that anyone else will like them either.

According to them, *they have no choice* when it comes to making friends and being accepted,

and because of this, they don't even try.

And just the fact that they're considered "loners" doesn't help matters much either.

It only confirms in their minds what they've been thinking all along.

That is ...

“I’m alone.

I have no friends.

Therefore,

I **must** be no good.”

What can be said
for people who think like this?

I liken their ***identity*** to a diamond
that is buried under a huge pile of dirt.

Even though the diamond is buried under all
that dirt, it **still** has extraordinary value.

The challenge is to dig for that diamond,

then cash it in for nice return.

Loners have extraordinary talent,

great characteristics,

and a lot of things to offer other people.

The town of Shelby lies within them just as much as it lies within anyone else.

Unfortunately, **it is buried under all that dirt.**

Oftentimes, it's dirt piled on by the person him/herself.

(See **Pages 81-93** to find out where **most** of this dirt comes from.)

And because it's hidden under all that dirt, no one ever gets a chance to see what kind of person the LONER really is.

So loners put themselves in a real tight box when it comes to making friends:

FIRST,

they don't even try to make friends because they don't think anyone is going to like them.

and

SECOND,

nobody comes their way to be friends with them not because they're bad people,

but because

their true identity

is buried under a pile of dirt.

It's hidden.

It's hard to make friends if nobody knows who you are.

To be honest with you, there's no great complicated, psychological solution to a loner's problem.

Loners have only two choices when it comes to doing something about their situation.

They can either
continue to do what they're doing
and keep
their diamond buried under a pile of dirt,

or

they can grab a shovel
and start digging.

For those interested in continuing
on the same path, nothing more can be said.

For those interested in digging,
there's a shovel on **Page 123**.

True, digging for that diamond
is going to be ***a lot*** of work.

After all, you're dealing with "***a lot*** of dirt,"
right?

But your diamond is definitely under there.

How bad you want to find it all depends
on how hard you're willing to look.

CHAPTER 2

DEPRESSION

Depression can be devastating …

especially if you don't understand
what causes it

and

what you can do to change it.

Although there are a number of reasons why people get severely depressed,

two main reasons stand out:

First is the inability of people
to **separate the bad things**
that happen to them in their lives

from the **amount of value** they already have
as individuals.

When people constantly take the blame
for all the bad things that happen to them
in their life,

feelings of hopelessness and depression
can't be too far behind.

This is called BLENDING,
and
you can find more information about it
starting on **Page 88**.

The second main reason for depression has to do with a **chemical imbalance** in the brain.

THIS IS NOT UNCOMMON.

Things like a serious change in sleeping habits, constant sadness, or crying for no reason

could be signs of depression caused by a chemical imbalance.

If you experience any of the above symptoms

or just feel constantly down much of the time and can't figure out why,

don't be afraid to ask someone to get you to a doctor for a checkup.

If you have to, *just go by yourself.*

You'd be smart not to put it off.

THERE IS SIMPLE MEDICATION TO HELP TREAT CHRONIC DEPRESSION

Statistics show that 90 percent of people suffering from depression ***respond favorably*** to medication.

That's 90 percent.

No matter what the cause of depression may be, one thing is for sure:

THINGS DO GET BETTER IN LIFE

IF

YOU WORK HARD TO SOLVE THE PROBLEMS THAT ARE CAUSING YOUR DEPRESSION

AND

YOU STICK AROUND TO SEE THE RESULTS.

This means you must ask for help from someone.

Some people turn to family members for help. Others turn to friends or teachers. Still others seek out God.

No matter who makes you feel comfortable, get to someone as soon as possible.

If you make the effort to work on your problems,

your life will get better.

Unfortunately, not everybody believes this.

There are those who feel life can never get better for them.

They think nothing will ever change for them no matter what they do in their life.

Elinore Wilson certainly felt this way.

The true story of Elinore Wilson is a good example of how some people place more value on *worldly success* and *personal recognition from others*

than they do on the *amount of value they have within themselves as individuals*.

Elinore Wilson was a struggling actress back in the 1940s. She wanted nothing more than to be a star,

a movie star.

She auditioned for every part that came her way, no matter how small it was. She did get some bit parts here and there, but never landed the role that would put her name up in lights.

The lack of progress in her career made her frustrated, angry, and – finally – seriously depressed. When drinking and drugs didn't help, she decided to end it all.

One day, Elinore trudged up to the top floor of a 40-story building in New York City,

walked out onto the roof,

and jumped off the edge,

falling to her death,

committing suicide.

Two days later, her agent received a phone call from a huge production company. The studio wanted Elinore to take the lead role in what would have been a major motion picture.

When the agent received the script, he was shocked at what he read.

You see, the role Elinore would have played was of a woman who was so depressed about her life that she climbed to the top of a building in New York City, walked onto the roof, and jumped off the edge, falling to her death, committing suicide.

Had Elinore sought the help she needed to work on her depression

and had she stuck around long enough to see the results,

she would have been the star she always had wanted to be.

Unfortunately, Elinore played out her role too soon.

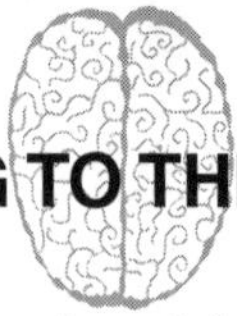

SOMETHING TO THINK ABOUT

If ***your best friend***
were constantly depressed,
would you try to help him/her deal with it ?

What would you do?

If ***you*** were constantly depressed,
would you try to help yourself deal with it ?

What would you do?

Would you do anything different for yourself
than you would do for your best friend?

CHAPTER 3

HOW TO FIND YOUR IDENTITY

As you've read in this book,

some people do strange things to find the town of Shelby in their lives.

But as you've also read,

the town of Shelby is not something
a person needs to search for.

It is something that already exists within us all.

The ability to be loved and accepted
will never leave you
no matter what other people
may say or do to you.

But what is it that you have
that makes this all possible?

What is it that draws people to you,

that makes them want to hang out with you?

What are some of the ***characteristics***
that make you
you?

WHAT'S GOOD ABOUT (your name)?

On the following two pages is a list of some of the more common **characteristics** a person ***may*** have that draw people to them.

They are the traits that **truly** define who a person is.

They are not based on how you **look**

or on what you **do** in the flesh body,

but rather on **who you are** as a person.

How many of these *characteristics* define who you are?

Keep in mind that you may have one, two, or even more of the following characteristics in your personality.

On the other hand,

you may not have any of them, but have others that are not listed.

The fact is,

there are many characteristics that define who a person is.

Which ones describe who you are?

WHO YOU ARE

You're a person ...

- ❑ who has a good *sense of humor.* You can make people laugh.
- ❑ who has *compassion* for other people, and you're not afraid to show it no matter who it's for.
- ❑ who is *"cool" under pressure.* You take things in stride no matter how serious the situation may be.
- ❑ who isn't afraid to *stand up for what is right* no matter what others may think and no matter what the consequences may be.
- ❑ who is *easygoing*, laid-back. People can mess around with you, and you don't take it personally.
- ❑ who is *loyal.* You're there for friends or relatives when they really need you.
- ❑ who *never quits.* You're a tough person. No matter how many times you "get knocked down" in life from family problems, personal problems, or problems with friends, you keep "getting up."
- ❑ who *treats others with respect.* You're not the kind of person who puts people down or talks about them behind their back.

You're a person ...

- ❑ who is *independent.* You're not led around by your friends, but rather you think for yourself. You're also a person who can get along fine by just hanging out with yourself. It's the kind of confidence others see and admire.

- ❑ who has *strong conviction* in what you believe in. Whether it be religion, values, social issues, whatever, you stick to your views no matter what other people may think.

- ❑ who has good *leadership skills.* When things get tough, people look to you for leadership as to what to do. You're the kind of person people can turn to for answers in tough situations. You think for yourself and don't allow others to influence your decisions.

These are just a few of the things that could make up who you are as a person. Are there others? There always are. If so, what are they? Give it some thought.

____

____

____

____

Once you've discovered what it is you have that other people can
and will

like about you,

you next need to understand
what it means to have

SELF-RESPECT.

After all, it's one thing to **know** who you are

and another to **respect and like** who that person is.

To learn how to do this, try the following:

Think of a person in your life
you **truly admire** or **love**.

This is a person you **really** look up to.

Got it?

Now answer this question:

How do you go about showing respect for this person you admire so much?

What kinds of things do you do?

Well, if you're like most other people,

you would never ***put this person down.***

If this person had a problem,
you would be there
for him/her.

You wouldn't do anything ***to hurt***
this person either mentally or physically.

If this person needed to have something
that would help better his/her life,
you would ***do what you could to get it.***

You would accept this person
as he/she ***is***.

If this person did something to
unintentionally hurt you,
you would have no trouble
forgiving him/her.

And

you wouldn't care what
other people thought about this person.

You know how much you like him/her,
and that's all that matters.

This is what it means
to have ***respect for others***,
especially for someone you admire so much.

This is also what it means
to have **respect for yourself**.

Go back and look at the list again.

You should be doing for yourself
what you would do for those people
you have the utmost respect for.

After all,

should you not have the same **admiration**
for yourself as you do for anyone else?

Aren't your characteristics
worthy of your respect?

Go back again to the previous page.

How many of those things do you do
for yourself?

How many of them ***don't*** you do,

but should?

CHAPTER 4

TRIVIA QUIZ

TRIVIA QUESTION NO. 1

Of the following people, who is the toughest person in your school?

A. The biggest, “baddest” football player on the team

B. The school bully

C. A boy named “Mike Tyson”

D. Someone who eats glass for lunch

E. The people some call “geeks”

The answer is simple: **E**.

The so-called "geeks" are the toughest people in your school, and the reason is obvious.

The so-called "geeks" in your school are people who have to endure a lot more mistreatment than most of the other students.

They get put down by people who are trying to make a name for themselves with their friends.

They get picked on by bullies who would think twice about picking on someone bigger than they are.

And oftentimes they're ignored by people who think they are "too good" to associate with

or even say "hi"

to someone who is "not their equal."

You have to be a pretty tough person to handle all this ***garbage*** and still keep an air of self-respect about you.

It would certainly be something
the ***name-caller***
or the ***bully***
or the ***conceited person***
would have a ***hard time*** doing.

My advice to the so-called "geek" is simple:

Hang in there.

That toughness you have in being able
to handle pressure will help you to become
a success in life one day.

Don't ever change from being
who you are as a person.

If you're not already
hanging out with somebody,

one day soon someone is going to realize
that there's a lot more to you than just the
"label" other people may put on you.

Without a doubt, one of the best-kept secrets in the world is just how tough the so-called "geek" or "nerd" really is.

Well, it's no secret anymore.

TRIVIA QUESTION
NO. 2

Some people do some pretty dumb things just to try to impress their friends.

What is the No. 1 negative FRONT used by teenagers to get attention from their friends?

A. Stealing

B. Doing drugs

C. Drinking alcohol

D. Putting other people down

E. Sticking a rubber hose up their nose and making water come out their ears

F. Skipping school

If you said "**D**,"

putting people down,

you're right.

TRIVIA QUESTION NO. 3

Why do people who put down other people pick on only those who are smaller or weaker than they are

and not on those who are bigger or stronger?

A. Because the small ones remind them of their younger brother or sister, and it's fun to pick on them.

B. Because the big ones remind them of their older brother or sister, and it's **not** fun to pick on them.

C. Because they like their face the way it is, and by picking on someone bigger, it might get rearranged.

D. Because someone with thick glasses and a briefcase couldn't possibly have a black belt in karate.

E. Because weaker people usually can't defend themselves. And since put downs are done mainly to get attention from friends,

what better way is there
to get attention than
to **use** someone who
can't defend him/herself?

Answers:

C and **E**

TRIVIA QUESTION
NO. 4

For which of the following situations do teenagers blame themselves the most?

A. Divorce

B. Parents' arguments

C. Abuse

D. Being put up for adoption

E. Death in the family

Answer:

A. Divorce

Although *parents' fighting* and *abuse* were a close second

and *adoption* and *death* ranked high,

divorce was clearly No. 1 in the

"It's-my-fault-
I-don't-know-what-I-did-
but-
I-must-have-done-something-wrong"

category.

It's really too bad that teenagers who blame themselves for divorce don't realize that divorce is about a

personality conflict
between two married people

and not about the children
they brought into this world.

BOOK CONCLUSION

Oftentimes,
the things we search for
most in life,

things like

the ability to

make friends,

be respected,

be accepted,

are things that have been with us all along.

All one needs to do is
use them.

Have any questions?
Want to talk about something in this book?

You can e-mail the author at

danc@lcp2.net.